ASIAN VOICES

FIRST GENERATION MIGRANTS

Mohammed Siddique

ASIAN VOICES

FIRST GENERATION MIGRANTS

NAFHESA ALI

Published by the University of Huddersfield

First published 2010
Text and images © Nafhesa Ali 2010

ISBN: 978-1-86218-089-5

Design & sketches by Athur Ali Mdes, MA (RCA)
Printed and bound by Riley Dunn & Wilson Ltd.
www.rdw.co.uk

Contents

Acknowledgements   6

Introduction   7

The University of Huddersfield   10

Heritage Lottery Fund   11

One   First Impressions   13

Two   Settling in Britain   25

Three   Labour in the 1960s   37

Four   Life in the Home   49

Five   Leisure   55

Six   Childhood and School Days   67

Seven   Food   77

Eight   Community, Culture and Religion   85

Nine   Identities   99

Glossary   105

Acknowledgements

Thanks are due to the Heritage Lottery Fund (HLF) and the University of Huddersfield's Centre for Oral History Research (COHR) in preserving the oral histories of the South Asian community in Huddersfield. I would like to thank all the people who shared their memories in the Asian Voices project and my apologies for the interviews I have not place in the book, due to space constraints; interviews are accessible within the University of Huddersfield Archives. I would like to thank all the people involved in the project, colleagues, students and Directors whose input and hard work has made the Asian Voices project a success. I would personally like to thank Dr. Stephen Kelly for the opportunity to manage the project and Professor Paul Ward and Stephen Dorril for their continued support.

The Huddersfield Examiner, Yorkshire Post and Sunrise Radio have been kind with their press coverage. A special thanks to Kirklees Council for the use of images in the website, www.asianvoices.org.uk and the Examiner for images within the book. I would also like to take this opportunity to thank all the schools who supported the project, Islamia Girls High School, Moor End Technology College, Spring Grove Junior School and Lindley (CE) VA Infant School; and thanks to Chris Webb who designed the learning resource packs.

Thank you to my parents Asghar and Balqees, for passing on their knowledge and heritage. My siblings Tayab, Athur and Faizah who with me, were the third generation. A special thanks to Athur whose talent has shaped the design of the book and who turned my photographs into wonderful sketches. Thank you to my husband Asif who has supported me through this journey and our beautiful children Anisa, Hakeem and Maariya. This book is written to preserve your generation's past and future heritage.

In memory of my grandmother, who sadly passed away during the completion of this book, but was the person I had the joy of recording first and for my grandfather, who was the first in line of four generations of our family to migrate to Britain in 1960 and is as active now in his 80th year, as he was then. A final thank you to everyone who donated photographs; there are too many of you to mention, but all of which give *Asian Voices* life, fifty years on.

Introduction

We each hold histories of our life experiences which largely lie undiscovered in the minds of each and every one of us. These stories hold valuable information to what life was like and the changes that have brought us to today. *Asian Voices* takes a community of individuals with untold histories from the Yorkshire town of Huddersfield and discovers how many uprooted their lives in search for riches. During the time of the British Raj in India, many Asians were told stories of the wealth and of better life in the British Empire, and thus searching for this dream, young men left their families and livelihoods to migrate to Britain.

The intention was never to stay, but to return after a few years. Young adults came to study and found themselves in manual labour jobs. Others came to retire in a country 'paved with gold', but found themselves starting over again in the industrial blackened town of Huddersfield in the 1960s. So why did they stay when the dream was so far from reality? Circumstance did not permit otherwise. The pressure to succeed became the root of embracing life in Britain. Men from successful families found themselves working endless late night shifts in order to survive. Farmers who had sold acres of land, now found themselves sharing homes with dozens of men, fighting for space to sleep. It took years for the first generation to settle and once they did families were sent for, which proved to be the beginning of new problems.

Wives and mothers faced huge cultural differences with regard to dress, culture, food and religion. With men working 12-hour shifts, women either moved away from their cultural norm and went to work or gradually became isolated due to the lack of understanding for their host community. These women went on to play the silent role of educator, teaching future generations their heritage, passing on their language, culture and religion, in the hope that it would not be lost in towns with make shift-mosques and temples in the homes.

For many, life in the 1960s was not easy and times were hard. Not having a bath to bathe in after your 12-hour shift in the textile mill, waking up in the middle of the night to visit the outhouse in your wellies and migrating from a country where many had never seen snow before. This first generation did however, overcome their struggles. There were good times to help them through; such as queuing all night to see the

Sikh Temple, Prospect Street, Springwood. Built in 1975.
View of Castle Hill in the background, which dates back to 1899.

Beatles at the ABC Cinema, now a Sainsbury's. There were movie Sundays, where everyone went to one of several cinemas to watch back-to-back Bollywood movies and finished the day with a meal in Bradford or trip to the seaside. Half a century later, the first generation migrants are truly settled in Britain, a country that is now characteristically multi-cultural. Places of worship are visible in most towns across Britain, curry has become a national dish and the mix of East and West fashion is visible in stores nationwide. The days of a foreign land have now become home.

It is now even more important to collect the memories of this first generation and preserve them for the future, as many of this first generation are now elderly and settled in life or have passed away. Their untold histories through *Asian Voices* will hopefully make you look twice at the man going to the local mosque or the families visiting the temple on a Sunday, it will help us understand why they worked hard in manual labour jobs and how their respect for the host community enabled them to break down language and cultural barriers; and perhaps, make you appreciate why they came to this country and the contribution they have made to its success and richness of life.

University of
HUDDERSFIELD

The University of Huddersfield

The University of Huddersfield was first established in 1825 as the Huddersfield Scientific and Mechanic Institute. The Institute continued to evolve and in 1914 a Technical Teachers College was located within the establishment, making it one of only four in the country. The Institute went on to be inaugurated as Huddersfield Polytechnic in 1970, officially designated by Education Secretary Margaret Thatcher in April, 1971. Following the Education Reform Act of 1988, in April 1989, the Polytechnic became the University of Huddersfield and was established as a self governing body, independent of the local Authority. The University of Huddersfield with an impressive range of undergraduate, post-graduate and research degrees has enabled thousands of students to achieve success, whilst its research has been of national and international importance.

The Centre for Oral History Research (COHR) was set up within the University in 2007 to coordinate the growing number of oral history projects within the School of Music, Humanities and Media. The Centre has since recorded hundreds of oral history interviews and continues to work on highly successful projects including, *Asian Voices*, Up and Under - Rugby League project, the Two-Minute Silence and the Cricket Heritage Project. First established by Dr. Stephen Kelly, the Centre is now run by Director Stephen Dorril, Author, Researcher and Investigative Journalist. COHR has worked in collaboration with the University of Huddersfield, the Heritage Lottery Fund (HLF) and Museums, Libraries and Archives Council (MLA) to fund oral history projects. Asian Voices was awarded £50,000 by the Heritage Lottery Fund and has been Project Managed by Nafhesa Ali.

Heritage Lottery Fund
(HLF)

The Heritage Lottery Fund (HLF) was set up in 1994 to distribute funds from the National Lottery to support a wide range of projects involving the local, regional and national heritage of the United Kingdom. In 2002 to 2003, the Heritage Lottery Fund committed over £360 million to more than 2,600 heritage projects. Among these projects were, histories of people and communities, historic buildings and streets, records and collections held in museums, archives and libraries, photographic collections, oral history in the form of people's memories and experiences, cultural and local traditions including languages.

The Heritage Lottery Fund takes on board a wide range of heritage projects to include the many different areas that have been and can be passed on from one generation to another. Since 1994, the Heritage Lottery Fund has awarded over £400 million to support educational activity. This has funded a wide range of large and small projects, which have delivered learning in the heritage settings. The Heritage Lottery Fund has become one of the most important funders of heritage learning in the United Kingdom and its grants have enabled a remarkable range of innovative and creative projects in the fields of both formal and informal learning to take place. Some of the most interesting projects have received support from this organisation, including *Asian Voices*, which set out to preserve the oral history testimonies from the South Asian community in Huddersfield.

heritage
lottery fund
LOTTERY FUNDED

First Impressions

Ashraf Ali, Newcastle, 1960.

Better living

I was born in December 1929 and I was thirty years old when I came to England from Toba Tekh Singh, Pakistan. We already lived in Pakistan during and after the partition and then I came to England in 1960. I lived in Newcastle for three years and I came to Huddersfield in 1963 and have lived here ever since. I came to work…it was easy then to get a passport and come to Britain, so I came because it was better living for the children, more money here. But when I came to Huddersfield it was very black and dirty, the stones were black because of the smoke from the mills. It was so different then…and the snow, I'd never seen snow before…I felt so cold.

Ashraf Ali

Why we came?

There were a few reasons, before me my father was here, he came in 1950 and we were young. We had a declaration so we came across in 1956. We've lived our whole lives in Huddersfield.

Balwant. S. Sandhu

World War II Soldier

My father was in the army in the Second World War, he was overseas. All his life he was away and then he retired in 1962. He used to get an army pension and wanted to rest, but my cousin who came to Britain in 1962, sent my dad a work permit. In those days getting a work permit wasn't very difficult, so he sent my father one and he came to England in 1964. Instead of retiring he began to work again, but this time in the textile mills.

Yaqub Masih

My own home

I came because there was a lot of poverty in Pakistan, to make a better life for my children, have a nice house, nice clothes and a comfortable life. Just to be able to buy books for my children. We couldn't even do that there. I was seventeen when my nannie got me married to my husband, who was already in England. When I came I felt sad that I was leaving my family behind, but happy too, because I would have my own home.

Balqees Akhtar Ali

Planes in the sky

The first time travelling by plane was really daunting. You'd see the planes in the sky, but on the ground they were massive big machines, DC-10s and had to stop three or four times on a journey…it was scary. When we got to England the first thing I noticed was that it was a long journey from London on the train. The planes only landed at London Heathrow then. It was so cold and the next day I noticed there was tons of snow. I was literally crying because I was so cold. It took weeks and weeks for me to figure out why I was here. I was crying at the weather, my friends and all of that.

Mohammad Haq

raditional wedding. Pakistan, 1963.

Ashraf and his siblings. Pakistan, 1956.

New environment

I was twenty five years old and I came here in 1962 to earn some more money because in our country Pakistan, it was just hand to mouth. I was a farmer there and farmed the land with my family. I heard people were going to England and there you could make a better life for yourself and your family. It wasn't easy for me to come over as the government only allowed metric pass and I was a farmer, but I managed. When I came I was really puzzled because of the language, the experience and the cold...it was a totally new environment. I was from the farming industry, but here, life was different. Everybody stayed at home and at the time I felt like a prisoner...I was so upset for weeks of getting here.

Fazal. R. Khan

16

Trees with pound notes

We had a misconception that we were going to England where there would be trees with pound notes. When I came I actually cried for a few weeks. Where I came from we were quite comfortable and I wanted to go back, but my friends and relations were here, so I stuck to it. I married a local girl and I've lived with two cultures for the last 46 years, but I never divorced myself from my culture or my people and I'm still proud that we're Indian.

Baldev Gill

Sabir and Margaret Hussain's engagement party, 1964.

One Bike and One Pound

I came to England in the 1950s with one bicycle and a pound in my pocket and that was all I had.

Parkash. S. Chima

This salute is a traditional greeting better known as a 'salaam'; meaning hello. Photo dates back to the early 1950s.

"Coal, coal, coal!"

I came to England on the 18th January, 1961 and I went straight to Glasgow, because I didn't know anybody and I had a relation there; so I stayed there for two months. I came to Huddersfield as there were no more jobs in Glasgow. We travelled by rail and when we came to Huddersfield, we disembarked of the train, there was an English lady waiting for us. She was married to a Pakistani and she helped us, she booked a taxi and we came to live in Water Street, number 22. The first thing I saw over here was that they used to sell coal, really big carriages loaded with coal and they would shout "Coal, coal, coal!" It was the first time I had seen anything like it.

Hanif Asad

Beautiful England

I had never travelled by plane before it was my first time and I remember sitting in the aeroplane and I felt lonely, I was even scared to move about. When I passed through London, it was strange. I had always heard that England was beautiful and I probably related that beautiful to the buildings, but I didn't like the buildings, especially the black stone and the terraced houses. As you entered the houses it was fine, but it was just the outside, it was all black and grey. It was due to the industry, but I didn't know that at the time.

Balvinder Kaur

Traditions

My father came as an economical migrant. My father came, my uncle came, and everybody came to work. There were traditions set up like that because there wasn't employment or anything back home. People thought if you go to England you will earn a better living, so my father decided to bring me here for a better future. I was so pleased to be going to England, it was seen as a kingdom. That's what I thought, but it wasn't like that. When I got here I had to work. I never had to work before…I was only fifteen.

Karam Hussain

Mr. and Mrs. Hanif Asad. Milnsbridge, 1967.

Meeting dad

I came to England in 1964, my father came in 1960 and when he came here he sold our house so he had enough money to buy the ticket to come across, so we stayed and went to live with my grandparents in Pakistan. I stayed there for four years so I could go to school and my mum went to live with her parents in a small village near by. We came to England in 1964...It was quite strange because I'd never seen an aeroplane before and it was the first time I had been in an aeroplane. It wasn't a big plane quite small and wasn't very stable either, kept going up and down, quite frightening actually. When we came to England because my father came when I was only four year old, I couldn't remember what he looked like and when we arrived at the airport, my mum recognised him and she was pointing him out to me up in the gallery waiting for us to come through the clearance. She was pointing him out to me and saying there's your dad...I could see who she was pointing to, but it wasn't until he came and picked me up that I realised it was my dad.

Asghar Ali

Traditional Family portrait picture taken in the 1960s

Snow in Pakistan

My elder brother was a Commission Officer in Pakistan and was stationed at Muri Hills 7449ft above sea level and it snows 13ft deep during winter, so I had experienced the snow before. It was no surprise.

Dr. Iqbal

A Frightening Experience

I came in 1962, as a student to study at Huddersfield Technical College. I knew somebody who lived on the same street as me in Pakistan who was already studying here. He had said I could get admission here as a student, so I did. When I came, it was frightening, I didn't know anybody and I cried for the first few nights.

Jamil Akhtar

Young men would leave their families behind for a better life in England.

Ahmed Ali, Blacker Road; 1964. Behind Ahmed to the left is Masjid Omar. Blacker Road is now renowned for its varied supply of Asian shops, including continental food stores, clothes shops, butchers and takeaways.

Cities and Houses

When we came, we took the taxi from the airport and it was late, probably around midnight when we left there. When we were in the car going back along the motorway I sat there and noticed there were lots of trees and it was very dark. They used to say England is a really nice place and I was thinking where are all the cities and houses they used to talk about.

Yaqub Masih

Chapter Two

Settling in Britain

Lachman Singh and Son, Springwood; 1962. Photo courtesy of the Huddersfield Examiner.

Fish and Chips

There were quite a few of us, about five or six people in one house. I think there were a few bedrooms, they were big houses. Our kitchen was in the cellar and there were probably four or five bedrooms. I had a single room to myself when I lived there and used to pay £1 a week. A wage was £5 to £6 pound, so £1 was a lot of money then, even though things were very cheap. At the time we had a ten shilling note and a ten bob-note. You could buy a weeks grocery on ten-bob, even then we had some change left. Fish and chips were only about two or three pence.

Sabir Hussain

Private School

I think there was a trend with people who came from India, they wanted to settle down and earn more money and then go back home. Some of them who were more educated, their priority was for the children to get an education and they admitted them back in India into private schools. They were sent back because we couldn't afford to pay for the child to be looked after here when they weren't in schools, there needed to be somebody around who could look after them and in my case there was no-body around; it was hard for us.

Balvinder Kaur

Village Barbers

The most difficult thing when we came here was that we had to do everything ourselves. In Pakistan, our meal was cooked by our mothers, if we had to shave and cut our hair we would go to a village Barbers, we didn't even know how to shave! We used to get up five in the morning, have a shave and a wash, prepare our own food, because we didn't know if it was halal or not; and in Pakistan most things were done sitting, even the cooking. Over here everything was done standing. Making the tea, making your meals, shaving and in the mills you'd stand for hours and then when we came back it would be another hour standing, making the evening meal and then we'd go to sleep. That was our only rest.

Hanif Asad

English

Even though I was well educated in India, people here couldn't understand my English and I couldn't understand theirs. They had a Yorkshire accent and I had an Indian accent.

Guru Datt Bali

Children would be sent back to live with granparents in Pakistan and India. Photo Pakistan, 1956.

Twenty Pakistanis, Twenty Indians

When I came here there were approximately twenty Pakistanis and twenty Indians in Huddersfield, six or seven houses. In every house there were five or six people who lived there, this was in 1956. The ones that came then, even Pakistanis were from India, Punjab. We were all from the same area.

Balwant. S. Sandhu

Starting over

When we first came everything was different. Culture was different, food was different, language was different and we were all young, sixteen to twenty-two, unless they were retired from the World War II army, they were all in their thirties and forties. There were no older people, we were all very young and most of us were unmarried. I went back to Pakistan and got married in 1966 and we spent up when we went back, so we started work and saving again and then brought the families over as living alone was very hard. When the wives came it was a lot easier as they could wash and make meals. The first five, six, seven years were very hard.

Hanif Asad

Shuaib, Tanveer and Asghar, 1973

Huddersfield was well known for its textile industry and craftmanship.

Famous Suits

In Pakistan the clothes were different, pants and shirts and so on. We did have them in Pakistan, but we didn't wear them very often, only in the city. When I was in college I only bought two suits and I wore my village clothes, shirt and sheets. When I came here I had bought my clothes from Pakistan and when I came here I realised they were slightly different styles, so I bought some from here too, to keep me warm. I don't know exactly which shops I bought them from, but my first suit was around £40. According to the wages then this was a lot of money and I still have the jacket. Huddersfield was famous for its suits.

Muhammad Ismail

Language

The main thing was language, not my language, but the people who came at that time. The majority, 90% couldn't speak the English language and they would ask the people who lived here if they would take them to the shop, so they could by food for them.

Fazal. R. Khan

Shamim Begum, Leeds Road, 1964

Dye House Manager

My dye house Manager arranged the mortgage for my house when I first came and it was very good, cheap rate. He helped me a lot. He settled the price for me, brought a lot of stuff from the shops and delivered it to my house. He was really helpful.

Muhammad Ismail

Buying a house

My father bought a house and suggested that I go and live there, but I didn't like the area. He bought me a house on Thornton Lodge Road, and I thought it was too cramped. I wanted to live on the outskirts, where there were plenty of trees and greenery and light, in the countryside. So I didn't like the idea and didn't want to go and live there. I was looking around and found a new estate that was being built on Norwood Road. It had a green belt on one side, which was quite nice because it was a wooded area. The houses were just being built and I decided to buy a house. My wife and I both came down and had a look and liked it so we put a deposit down on of £100. The house was going to cost us £14,000, in those days you could buy a three bedroom house for less than a £1000 and that was quite expensive for me, but it was within my limit. After putting down £700 as deposit, with the rest as mortgage, I was able to buy the house. We did ask ourselves could we afford it, could we not? But we decided to take the risk.

Asghar Ali

One and a half bedrooms

I came to England in 1964. It was cold. There wasn't any snow, it used to snow, but it didn't on that day. I came by myself, three of my children and my two nephews as my children were very young. My husband met me at the airport and took me home. He had bought a house on Leeds Road in Huddersfield. It was a small house one and a half bedrooms, but it was just me and him, and three small children so it was fine.

Shamim Begum

Women

When my mum came over she struggled quite a lot because in Pakistan the women have a very sheltered life, they don't have to go out and work and they had to have a male presence with them when they did go out. Dad was away at work so much she was expected to go to work as well, it affected her. She found the cultural difference between the British society and the Pakistani very hard to come to terms with and she used to keep herself in the house. I think the first generation really suffered.

Mamuna Karim

Women passing their time at the allotments. George Avenue, Birkby; 1968.

Frightened by the words

I was so reluctant to speak English, I started to learn a little bit, but I was very shy. I think it was because English was a totally new language and I was frightened that the words I would speak would be wrong and that they would laugh at me. So probably for those reasons I was a bit introvert, but I started speaking English eventually.

Mohammad Haq

Ahmed Ali, outside his home on Macaulay Road, Birkby; 1971.

The Struggle for Independence

Because of all the problems in the early 1960s, the Indian Workers Association was set up for all South Asians and Afro-Caribbeans. We were a lead organisation, fighting for rights in temples, mosques and in people's houses. We went shoulder to shoulder with all who were sympathisers, not just Asians, offering a shoulder to cry on telling people if we can't help you there are others who can. The people involved in the struggle for Independence in India were the ones who set up organisations like IWA, Hindus and Muslims, who came to this country for studies…We were proud that at least we had links with people who were involved in the struggle for independence and achieved it, even though we had to achieve it when we came here.

Baldev. S. Gill

A war between Pakistan and India

I was born in Punjab, which is already in Pakistan, but I was called back in 1965, when there was a war between Pakistan and India, and I was called back as Captain. I was already working here as a Research Chemist, so I said, "No, I can't". The war between Pakistan and India only lasted a little while and by the time the letter went back and forth the urgency had disappeared.

Dr. Iqbal

Dr. Iqbal came to Huddersfield in 1963.

St. George's Square, 2010.
The Railway Station in St. George's Square dates back to 1847.

The Thought of Returning

My father's three elder brothers came first and they all came to live in Huddersfield. The earliest one came in 1952 and they settled in Huddersfield and lived on Carlton Street in Hillhouse. My father came in 1963 and was twenty seven years old. He was the youngest of seven brothers and two sisters. He told me that when he came to St. George's railway station the first thing he noticed was how black everything was and that the air was heavily polluted. He began work in a foundry and within weeks his hands were scarred from working with hot metal all day and he hated it here. He wanted to go back to Pakistan, but his brothers persuaded him to stay. He then got married and five years later his wife came over and they had me, their son. The thought of returning had then turned into a dream for my dad, as he had thought he would only stay for a few years and return to Pakistan, but it just wasn't so.

Mehboob Khan

Chapter Three

Labour in the 1960s

Ashraf Ali, Bus Conductor; 1961.

No Jobs for Clerks

In Pakistan, I was clerk in the Irrigation Department and I was educated to metric level. I worked in the Irrigation Department for ten years and then came to England. I went to Newcastle first where I worked on the buses as a bus conductor and in Huddersfield I worked in the textile mills mainly. It was okay, because there were no jobs for clerks, women did that job and there was less money in it. You could do overtime in the mill. We would do shifts, some would go to work during the day, then some would go during the night; and that's how we lived in the house too. There were ten people in the house all living together. I got my own home in 1964 when my wife and children came over, but I worked in textiles for 25 years ...a long time.

Ashraf Ali

Work or School

I was fifteen years old and straight away when I came I had to work. I worked in the textile mills it was a tragedy really. My father wanted me to go to the school and they said, "You're fifteen years old, the school will not accept you, you have to find a job." That was the advice given to my dad and I applied for a job and got one straight away. It was very hard work textile work, I worked on the grinding machines and then I worked as a spinner. When my grandfather discovered I was working he didn't accept it. He didn't send me to England to work at that age, so my grandfather called me back to Pakistan. I ended up dividing my time during the year here and there.

Karam Hussain

Earning money

When I started work it was quite different and difficult for me, because in Pakistan I was a school teacher and here I was a mill worker. It was not very difficult, just different. I was very happy, the first week I got about £8 wage for 40 hours and after two weeks the mill was so busy I worked overtime. Including overtime, my wage was about £15 to £16. After that the standards went up and the pay went up and up and up. In 1984 I think my wage was £134. The labour job was very hard, but I never found it hard. In Davis Dyers, my first job in a dye house, I was placed in the scrubbing house and the dying department. After that all my jobs were textile work, twisting and winding.

Muhammad Ismail

Textiles

My brother was already here in Huddersfield, in 1953 or 1954, and he encouraged me to come over here even though I had a job in India. I came over here in 1966 and I didn't expect to work hard in this country and at the time the job I got was in textiles. Everybody had a job there because Huddersfield was mainly a textile town, so I went to work in the mills. I didn't like the job and I moved to some other job and that work was even harder. I used to work on night shifts seven nights a week, sometimes you'd do a lot of over time and it was just something you got used to.

Mohan Sokhal

Ramsden Mill, Linthwaite.

Cotton balls

I went with someone for a day or two and after that never worked again. I didn't like the men, it was full segregation in Pakistan even from uncles and cousins and it was a lot more then. So when I went to work I was embarrassed. I worked for two weeks and it was the Christian neighbour who took me. She said, "You're at home all day, so come to work". I went and we made balls, cotton balls took them off and put them in your lap, it wasn't hard work, but I didn't realise that. I did that for a week. I didn't like it, the men would come round and ask if I had finished and I would stay quiet. The neighbour thought I didn't speak so she'd say, "if you want to work come, if you don't, then don't come." So I never went back and I left work. Even my husband didn't say anything about going back to work, normally they'd say go back, but he didn't. So I never went back to work again.

Shamim Begum

Mohan Sokhal came to Huddersfield in 1966.

Hepworth Mill

I worked at Hepworth Mill. My first job was as a Pipe Maker and only a few people in Huddersfield worked there. They only had six Indian people before me and I was the seventh on night shift. They didn't have any during the day. Who-ever started before me had only been there for six months. When you worked it was straight forward, it was really different then than now. At the time we had problems with English and everything in general and it was hard, but we still managed to find work.

Balwant. S. Sandhu

Case of pound notes

No-body thought they'd come here and work five shifts. They thought they'd get a case full of pound notes just by coming here. It never happened because whatever you earned a week you paid and at the end of week. You were lucky if you had any money left, you earned seven to eight pound a week and that was it.

Baldev. S. Gill

T. A. Corkings

I came mainly to study and in Pakistan I heard that the field I was more familiar with, electronics, I could expand my knowledge and get a good job in England. At first I studied three nights and worked during the day so I could get by. The first job I did, the name of the firm was T. A. Corkings. They used to make hydraulic rings for aeroplanes and ships. I was very good technically and I made many of the rings. I checked the rings and could say whether they were good rings or bad rings. That's why the firm owner was very taken with me and thought I was a good asset to the firm. It was on Old Leeds Road, near the back of the Sports Centre. My job wasn't that difficult really, I used to have an iron mould and you'd put the rings into it and put it into a heater to cook them and make them stronger. There was a system on the machines, when the ring was ready it would come off, I was doing that for about four years. It was quite an interesting job, but I didn't want to do that my whole life.

Sabir Hussain

Water Works Offices, Water Street, Springwood. Dates back to 1828.

43

The weather

The weather...it used to snow a lot. There was so much snow and you had to go to work to the mills. You'd get there two, three hours late. It was really difficult... for weeks at a time it would stay and not melt. Now it doesn't snow like that, it would be frozen on roofs like a glass sheet for many, many weeks. We've come out of a lot of difficult times.

Mohammad Siddique

Fighting for wages

I got a job at Waterhouse Brothers, a small firm as a weaver and that fellow worked for a Commission Agent. Most of the time he was a heavy drinker and we'd have to fight for our wages. We knew where he went for a drink so we used to chase him and get our wages from him. I was so fed up, so I looked for another vacancy and got a job at Moxen Brothers at Kirkburton. It was a very good firm and I went there in July, it was a good day and we sat outside and got talking. He said, "I like you and want to employ you, but the trouble is that I think it will cause a lot of trouble, because you are a coloured man and will be the first Asian here." So I told him I understood and left. I started working somewhere else and he called me back and said, "Come back and I'll see to it that you get a job." So I did, I went back.

Hanif Asad

Mathematics

I worked for a year in a laundry and I always thought that this work isn't for me and the girls who were working there applied for a job in Gibbs, an American firm, and I applied for a job there too and got it. It was just packing and boxing toothpastes and on the fifth week I was coming down the stairs during lunchtime and some people were doing some mathematics calculations. I stood on the stairs and said "What are you doing?" and I said "No, No this is like this," and did the calculations in a few seconds. After a few days, I was called by the manager and I was placed on another job, weighing products and filling sheets. It was much better and it made me feel really good as I could go to higher management and discuss things. I was also put on a higher wage. My husband was bringing £14 home and I started earning £36 a month and I thought, "Oh, this is really good."

Balvinder Kaur

Zahida and clasmates celebrate a 100th birthday; 1975.

Happy Medium

My story is a little different, I was qualified back home with two degrees, a bachelor's degree and Masters in Chemistry and I got a job straight away Research Chemist. I came in November 1963 and found a job in January 1964. Whilst I was working as a Research Chemist at L. B. Holliday and company on Leeds Road, they manufactured dice, coloured dice, I had applied for a job as a teacher, as professionally I was teaching chemistry in Faislabad in Pakistan and started working as a teacher in 1965 here and did that for five years. I taught at St James Grammar School, O' Level Chemistry as it was called then and taught newly arrived children from Pakistan and India in a reception centre in Spring Grove School on Water Street in Springwood. It was a happy medium, teaching Chemistry at the Grammar School and teaching newly arrived students social skills.

Dr. Iqbal

45

Bus Conductor

Whoever was educated only got one job and that was a Bus Conductor, if you were like us, farmers, you'd work in the foundry and our life was hard.

Balwant. S. Sandhi

Injury at Work

My granddad came in 1937, my dad came in 1954 and I came in 1958. I was 18 years old when I came and I started work in John Cotton, Mirfield. We all lived in Huddersfield but worked there because my uncle worked there. We would get the bus then, no many people had a car and I would work 12-hour shifts. After that I went to a foundry and worked there in the fitted shop floor. The reason I left John Cotton was because the shifts were long and it took time to get to Mirfield, but I did return to John Cotton a the shifts went down to eight hours, but I got paid for twelve. I eventually had to stop because I got injured. You had to put oil in a cylinder and mix it with water and spray so the wool doesn't fly about for the pads for sofa's and duvets; you'd spray them so they'd fold. They cylinder had oil in it, it went to three or four machines and someone put more water in it and forgot to turn it off. The oil spread on the floor and I slipped I couldn't get up. I was off for a few months and then that was it.

Dev. S. Uppa

Just a Holiday

I had just come for holiday, I wasn't intending to stay for long. I started to work on the buses and I thought I would only be there for six to eight months and I was still there twenty years on.

Jamil Akhta

No such jobs

I came in 1963 and at the time they were doing an employment voucher where you could come to work in England. I applied for a voucher and I received a voucher for Senior Stenographer, but when I came here I realized there were no such jobs here for me because those jobs were only for women. I was a bit stuck then as I had come for better life and my first job ended up in textiles as a weaver at K. M. Brown in Newson

Guru Datt Ba

Ashraf Ali, Huddersfield Bus Driver, 1965.

Chapter Four
Life in the home

Balqees at home with her sisters in Bhawalpur, Pakistan, 1973.

Learning a range of skills

We didn't work, we stayed at home in Pakistan. Mum said that you should stay at home and not go out. In Pakistan, girls stayed at home reading the Quran, learning about Islam, learning Islamic stories, doing the housework, sewing, knitting, crochet, learning everything. If we said we didn't want to do that they'd say, "learn everything because you never know when you might need it in your life." We learnt not because we were going to use it, because we had too learn everything; embroidery, needlework, knitting cooking chapatti, curries, cleaning. We learnt everything and I used it when I came to England.

Balqees Akhtar Ali

Abdul Majeed and baby, 1964.

British vs Tradition

We had to live two lives. We tried to lead a British cultural life outside of the house, but inside of the house we immediately changed our clothes and had to be Asians and lead the Asian life. It was hard for us, but it became the norm. We didn't think we had to do it we just did it. We had one kind of life in the house and a different one outside of the house.

Mamuna Karim

"People came and went..."

At home, I'd just do the housework and look after the children. The days just passed like that. I mixed with the neighbours, the number ten and number eleven houses. People came and went. The houses were old and needed cleaning, the wives didn't want to do that, so they moved and in those days the houses were cheap. In the hundreds, £500, £1000; nothing more than that.

Shamim Begum

Saturday, Shopping Day

Everyone who came, knew very little English, most people who came were farmers. When I came, I knew a little English and where we lived in the houses, there were seven to eight men in one house. So we distributed the work, somebody cooked the curries, somebody else made the chapattis and my job because I knew a little English, was to buy the food... Saturday was always shopping day.

Balwant. S. Sandhu

Meeting people

I came to this country in 1969. When I came, to this country, I was a housewife and when I came from India I was pregnant so quite soon after, my son was born, so I looked after my children here; I was only twenty years old. I did meet other ladies, say "hello", like this... but I don't know, there wasn't a relationship. We didn't know about things like that, I didn't have many friends – but we'd make new friends easily and just ask them, where do you live? Where are you coming from? India. Which part of India? Like this, we talked to each other openly.

Satwant. Samra

Daughters

Friends were buying small businesses and we thought we could do that, so we bought a shop. It was good for a few years, but we were making little money from the shop. Then my other daughter was born, so I had the opportunity to stay at home looking after my daughters, whilst working in the shop. It was comforting that I was at home.

Balvinder Kaur

Portrait of two sisters in traditional salwaar kameez and 'English-style' dress, often homemade by mothers.

Fish Curry

We got Saturday and Sunday off, we had to go shopping and clean the house. We were tenants, but we had to clean the house and cook ourselves and we were all men. We used to cook fish, there wasn't much fish, but we used to put curry powder into it and make a sort of curry. We used to cook that quite a bit and have it a few days a week.

Sabir Hussain

Pint or Two

You only had Sunday off, the other days, six days a week you'd work, five and a half days everybody worked day or night shifts and you'd work Saturday too. On Sunday, because our families weren't here we would wash our clothes do everything ourselves and at dinner time have a pint or two at the pub, but the other days you'd be at work.

Balwant. S. Sandhu

Living in the Jungle

My grandfather used to say to me that where they built their house in Khasmir, they were more or less living in a jungle and they still had to work and earn to live there. He told me a story of when his dad went to get a beam for the house from a tree and there was a lion drinking water at the water hole. He came home and had to put the wheat grinder against the door because they had no locks, and they were big heavy things made out of stone. He was afraid of the lion coming into the home.

Karam Hussain

Different lives

I called for my wife thirteen years after I had come. It was the same for everyone at the time. We came alone because we were not sure of what would happen to us when we came. When I realized life was easier here I saved up some money and applied for her to come. When she came here she enjoyed living here with me and the children. There was an Asian lady who lived next to us, so she had company when she came; they're lives were so different to ours.

F. R. Khan

Chapter Five

Leisure

Sabir and Margaret Hussain, Lands End, 1978.

Sunday Drive

The first car we had was an Avon Minx, it was quite a good car. We bought that at the garage near KFC. On weekends we used to go all over, on a Sunday. Saturday was shopping day, cleaning day, but Sunday was relaxing day. Usually we'd go to Bradford and have a good breakfast, potatoes and chickpeas and mango pickle. That was only a snack in the morning, for the main meal we used to go to the Sweet Centre, which was in Bradford. They used to have a restaurant and everybody would go there regularly, it was a long time ago in the 1960s. When we'd finished there, we'd go to the pictures and see Pakistani and Indian films. Sometimes we went to Blackpool or Scarborough. On Sunday we enjoyed ourselves.

Sabir Hussain

Empire Cinema, John Williams Street, Huddersfield. Dates back to 1913.

No time to go anywhere

After working so many hours there wasn't a lot of time to go anywhere. I didn't have any relatives here and my friends were not local, so with my children being young, I had to look after them and provide for their education. I was just making money and saving money for my children's education. There were a lot of cinemas and people used to go there. One was called Empire, by the outdoor market, another was near the university. I did go to the Empire. Mostly people from round here went to Bradford to watch the films. Here, there were people from Pakistani and Indian backgrounds both going together to the movies and we all enjoyed them.

Mohammad Ismail

Three movies for the price of two

On Sunday, the whole family would go out because there was no other entertainment and people would just wait for the weekend. On Saturday, we would do a bit of shopping, go for baths, but on Sunday we would make sure everybody was at the cinema. They used to have an ABC cinema here in Market Place, in Huddersfield and there was also the Empire. That was people's entertainment, they would spend the whole day watching two movies and if there were three on, they'd be over the moon at getting three movies for the same price. Then on Monday we would go back to work again.

Yaqub Masih

Designed by Stocks and Sykes. The cinema seated 796 and often played Bollywood movies in the 1960's.

Beatles Concert at the ABC Cinema, 1961. Photo courtesy of the Huddersfield Examiner.

The Beatles

The main thing was that people welcomed me, the spirit people used to have. In pubs, there were different rooms, piano rooms, pool rooms, people used to laugh and talk with each other and we didn't drink at all, just enjoyed ourselves. In the 1960s there were all these music groups. I saw the Beatles, saw them all at the ABC Cinema where the old Sainsbury's is in town. It was bigger than the London Palladium. I saw everyone there, the stage was so huge. I remember when I went to see the Beatles, the queue was backing from the Police Station up the winding street right to there. I was there in the evening and I got the ticket at 11am in the morning. The show was the next week. I stayed there all night. The ticket was about 15 shillings or something, about 75p. The point is that if it was too much, no-one could afford it. The ordinary clubs no-one paid anything. There were comedians and musicians and all sorts. All the top acts used to come. They were really fantastic, honestly.

Sabir Hussain

Bradford

When I first came, I didn't have any free time at all. I worked seven days and seven nights. Whenever I had a day off I go to Bradford to have a tandoori roti and go to the cinema. That was my leisure in those days. Going to Bradford and having food in a restaurant it was a treat and the cinema, well it was to be honest always full. When you went, first of all a lot of people would know you and when you saw the Asian movie it was tremendous. In those days, where we came from we hadn't seen a movie or anything like that before, so it was new to us.

Karam Hussain

A Candle

The Huddersfield baths at Clare Hill, that's where everybody used to go, it was even like a social outing. After I came over the following day my cousin said, "we're going for a bath," so he took me…it was really strange. It's totally different now as they all want en-suite in every room. At that time, even toilets, if you had to get up at night you would have to go outside, whether it was raining or not. It would probably be dark in the toilet as well, unless you had a candle there.

Yaqub Masih

Inside Cambridge Road Baths. Dating back to 1931, the baths were used for swimming and would be boarded over to be transformed into a dancing stage in the evenings. The baths also held facilities for bathing, which was often a social meeting place.

Indian Workers Association, Old South Street, Springwood.
Established in 1965.

Indian Workers Association

There was discrimination, you know in the work place and other places like in the pubs because they were no families or very few families just men and when they came back from work they wanted to talk to people, friends and the only places they could get together was pubs. When I started going to pubs, there was a lot of discrimination and we were not allowed into certain pubs. If we tried to go in we would be told to go away, so we set up the Indian Workers Association to work against this discrimination in 1965. The more people that came over from India the bigger it grew and the bigger the need for support.

Mohan Sokhal

Chimney, Springwood.

Learning to Drive

I learnt to drive the car, that was the first thing I did. There was a car parked at home and I had to drop my sister-in-laws off at school, it was hard. Sometimes, we would walk or go on the bus and I didn't like the bus as I was brought up in the home in Pakistan and wore the burqa. I didn't like getting the bus, men could see me, so I learnt to drive the car. I was so determined and I passed my driving test first time round.

Balqees Akhtar Ali

Mamuna in her dad's car, 1969.

Men would dress smartly for a day
out to the pictures, 1962.

Pakistani Pictures

On Sundays, we used to have the day off. On Saturday, we would work until 7pm and
the only entertainment we had was going to the pictures to watch Pakistani movies and
they'd show us two pictures each time on a Sunday. Where Primark is now, there used
to be Curzon cinema and there was Majestic cinema where Tesco is now and the
Cannon cinema across from Kingsgate. There was another cinema where the Hindu
temple is as well. ABC cinema, where Sainsbury is...There were lots in Huddersfield,
it was they only was of socialising because we could see each other and everyone
would come and we would go for coffee or a cup of tea afterwards.

Hanif Asad

Ahmed Ali (right) with friend in Greenhead Park, 1964.

Movies for Half a Crown

There was the Empire cinema next to the open market and almost everybody during those years went to see the cinema on Sundays. There used to be two and a half hourly films shown every Sunday for half a crown. For six months, I went there continuously with friends, people from my house, but I gave it up because I found out that all the films had the same plot, the same story, the same actors, similar songs, so I didn't go again.

Dr. Iqbal

Good Friends

In our free time we would look forward to Sunday and go to the pictures in Bradford or get together to play cards. Sometimes we would go to the pub, I know culturally Pakistanis wouldn't go to the pub, but at that time we all went, we were all good friends with each other and we would all go just to socialise.

Baldev. S. Gill

No Free Time

We didn't have free time we would work seven days a week. In the morning we would have to make our food, roti and daal, there weren't any women then. We would finish work at night and then you wouldn't have time to cook or do anything. We were never free to go out.

Dev. S. Uppal

Trip to the Seaside

Because we had uncles and aunts that lived in Huddersfield that was our social life. We visited cousins and they were our social events. Holidays would be spent at relatives houses and they would come to our house. So you didn't feel as if you were missing out on anything because you had that close extended family. For our family holiday out, Dad used to take us to Blackpool, every year we'd go to Blackpool. We went on the beach, in the sea and as we got a bit older we started going on the games and rides. When we were younger they just used to go on the beach and have a picnic, they'd cook food and take it with them... but we all used to get together and the whole family would go.

Rehana Tanwir

Chapter Six

Childhood and School Days

Street Games; Tayab and Athur Ali, Woodthrope Terrace, 1979.

Standing guard

As far back as I can remember we had to study and if we were caught playing out we were in big trouble. One of us would always stand guard to watch out for dad coming around the corner at the bottom of the street.

Mamuna Karim

Street Games

We lived on St. Stevens Terrace which has now been demolished and some new flats have been put there. There were mainly Asian families living there, although there were some English families living there as well. We used to gather in the street and play games. Batman used to be on and that used to be our favourite programme and also Superman comics, they were our favourite comics. There used to be a Salvation Army hut just nearby there, which has now been bought out and is now a mosque. We used to go to the Salvation Army hut in the evenings and we used to enjoy playing games there, because they used to have all sorts of activities going on. Basically, there were mixed people there, people from English homes and people from Asian homes, and we got on quite well there. We used to enjoy that, because it was kind of a pastime. People were quite friendly, actually. Occasionally, I would go to the house of one of my English friends and her mother would offer tea and biscuits, quite enjoyable, quite nice actually. I didn't experience any negativity at that time.

Asghar Ali

Mamuna, Rehana and Zahida, 1970 . (Above and across).

Childhood

As kids we were really happy and playful and enjoying life, but thinking back it's quite different. We had an outside toilet and it was freezing, too cold for anyone to go out and use the toilet in winter. There wasn't a proper bathroom in the house, there was a bath in the cellar, which had an old gas geyser next to it which was erratic and it didn't work properly. Whenever you were fully immersed in water it decided go off just like that.

Mehboob Khan

Pretend Play

From school we would go home, we wouldn't go out. We were allowed to play in the garden but we couldn't go out onto the street. We were allowed to play at home and we had a swing and a bike, in those days that was quite novel to have big items. We didn't have a lot of toys and we didn't have dolls but we'd make our own. I remember rolling up towels to pretend they were dolls.

Rehana Tanwir

Probationary School

I went to a probationary school in Springwood. That's where I had a lady teacher, Mrs. Verma. I was in her class and all the boys and girls from overseas, Indian, Pakistan were all together. This was also the first time I saw the Indian community because I had not seen television before. My grandfather used to talk about Indian partition, Indian Sikhs wearing turbans. This was the first time I'd seen a teacher with a turban on, so I realised what the Sikhs looked like. One of the funny things there was one of the girls who started writing English from right to left because you're used to writing Urdu from right to left, so we'd laugh at things like that.

Mohammad Haq

Racism

At that time we didn't realise why they were being racist towards Asian people we just felt they didn't like us we didn't understand why they didn't like us we were too young to understand that, but we just knew that when a load of skinheads ran towards you, you ran in the opposite direction and it happened on quite a frequent basis. I remember in High School, I was being chased by skinheads who looked quite fierce, some actually had bomber jackets, Doc Martin shoes and lots of studs and earrings and tattoos, and they were chasing us around the long and very extensive fields that the school had, but we didn't realise why they were chasing us, we just thought it was a bit of fun and we were very good at running. They never caught us so we thought that was alright, they were all smoking and out of breath, but that's an experience that kids don't have these days and hopefully not in Huddersfield.

Mehboob Khan

In-line with tradition

I remember in school, because it was the majority were English, I was wearing trousers and because girls used to wear skirts a teacher said to me, "you shouldn't wear trousers." There was no school uniform, but she was just quite negative. I think because then trousers were for boys. I don't know whether that had an impact on me because I started wearing skirts and I started sewing my own clothes. My older sister wore Asian clothes and I was the first one to start wearing English clothes. But I used to make sure I was fully covered, which was in tradition with the culture and religion, so my dad didn't say anything.

Rehana Tanwir

Spring Grove School, Bow Street, Springwood. Dates back to 1879.

The Cane

If you were naughty the teacher could send you to the headmaster and the headmaster would take out his cane, ask you to put your hand out and hit you with the cane. I remember being punished myself once, because we went to the swimming pool and we were on a double decker bus. The window was open and there was a branch sticking inside, I was about to push the branch out of the bus when the teacher came upstairs and saw me. He thought I'd pulled the branch and anyway he said, "right, I'm going to send you to the headmaster." He sent me to the headmaster and the headmaster asked me what I'd done. I said, "There was a branch and I was trying to push it out." I don't think the headmaster believed me. He asked me to put my hand out and slammed me with the cane. It was really painful. That was enough to put me off doing anything wrong.

Asghar Ali

Captain of the Football Team

At school, I was captain of a football team for a couple of years and thoroughly enjoyed it. The Headmaster David Chambers was a brilliant teacher, but very strict. We used to have corporal punishment then if anybody did anything wrong.

Mohammad Haq

Mohammad Haq, football team captain at Spring Grove Junior School, 1967.

72

MP. J. P. Mallaliey visiting Spring Grove School, 1963. Photo courtesy of the Huddersfield Examiner.

Girls don't wear Trousers

I remember in school, I was wearing trousers and because girls used to wear skirts a teacher said to me, "You shouldn't wear trousers." There was no school uniform, but she was just quite negative. I think because then trousers were for boys. I started wearing skirts and sewing my own clothes. My older sister wore Asian clothes and I was the first one to start wearing English clothes, but I used to make sure I was fully covered which was in line with tradition, my dad didn't mind then.

Rehana Tanwir

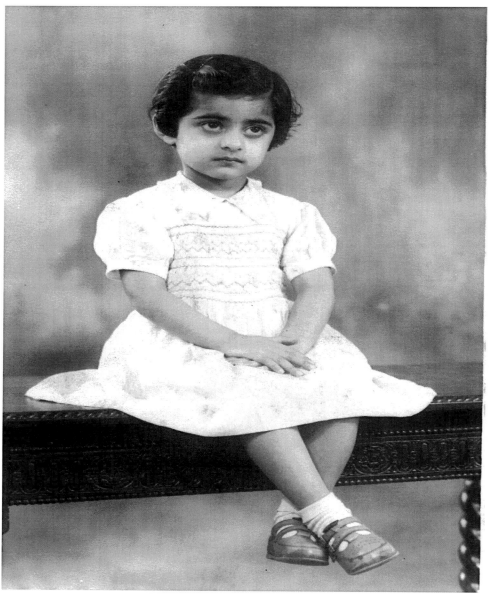

Girls would dress smartly in 'English' clothes to have their portraits taken, which would often be sent back to Pakistan to show how well the families were doing in England; Photo, 1959.

Learning to Read and Write

It was really different for me. Where we lived in India, we have a farm and when we go to school we only learnt to read and write and then we'd go back to work. We didn't go into higher education because we didn't want to do a job in the office. We had our land, so we didn't need a lot of education.

Balwant. S. Sandhu

Just Dessert

The school meal was six pence a meal. I never ate the main meal and I only had the sweet; rice pudding, custard and apple pie. I never touched the main meal even though it was alright, I just didn't like it. We told the schools not to give our children pork and not to allow mixed swimming for the boys and girls...just cultural things they didn't know about.

Dr. Iqbal

School Bus

From 1965 onwards, there were some obstacles for the Asian community. In 1967 and 1968, a lot of families came to England and there were a lot of children who came. The council put them into Rawthorpe School, put them into buses and sent them there. We were not happy about that and we said that the children should mix with the English children. We had a few meetings with the Councillors and all of a sudden, somebody in the council wanted to look at it and questioned if it would work better if the children went to the local school. So they put Fartown people into Fartown School and Newsome children into Newsome, rather than ferrying them across town to Rawthorpe. There the children would think they were still in Pakistan and India.

Piara. S. Salona

Chapter Seven

Food

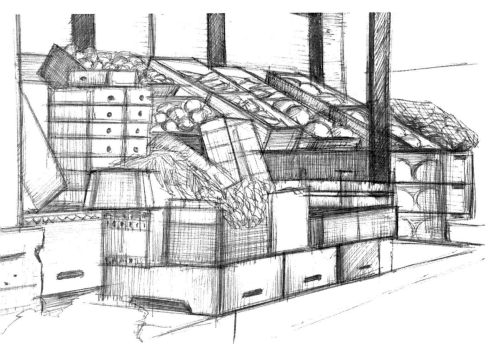

Continental Food Stores, Blacker Road, Birkby.

Shops

Its really nice now, you couldn't buy things before, there were only a few shops and you would have to go to across town to buy things. Now, there are lots of Pakistani shops across Huddersfield where you can buy Asian food things like massalas, halal meat, chappati flour and rice. It was difficult before, but now they're everywhere.

Balqees Akthar Ali

Sabir and Margaret outside Woolworths, Victoria Lane. 1964.

Rationing

Food...we only got two packets of flour and only got lentils. Not like now and only cauliflower. Meat was no problem as there was a farm in Milnsbridge and on a Saturday two or three of us would go to the farm and get some chickens, have it skinned down there and cook it at home. Meat wasn't a problem. The problem was we couldn't get butter and basics. One person was allowed two packets a month. When we came they started, my father got half a pound of butter a month, they were rationing sugar as well. After that you got some flour and you could make chapatti and at the time there were very few Asians, so there weren't many shops.

Balwant Singh Sandu

"Cook, cook, cook..."

It was like this you know, we'd buy the shopping from Woolworths, where the things were on the shelf you could just pick them up, take them to the counter and pay for them there...One guy went and said "cook, cook cook". He went for eggs.

Piara Singh

Halal Chickens

After a few years, there were a couple of shops where we could get halal meat on George Street. There was a Pakistani shop there, but before that we used to halal our own chickens. We used to go to a farm to get chickens, buy the chicken and take the meat from there. Sometimes, we used to do it in the back garden. We'd make them halal and skin the chicken and all the chicken skin and fat we used to burn in the fireplace! To us, it was the main source of meat. Otherwise you couldn't buy any because you didn't know if it was halal.

Sabir Hussain

"Smelly Curry."

At that time, it was also a new experience for English people with the Asians coming in and if they smelt a curry being made next door they thought, 'oh it smells'. But eventually if you have English neighbours we would say, "would you like to eat some as well." People just started getting used to it.

Yaqub Masih

Halal Fried Chicken Takeaway, Trinity Road, Huddersfield.

Carefree

We went to Birmingham once, when the motorway opened. We stopped on the side of the motorway and the policeman came and asked us if we had broken down. We told him we hadn't and we were eating our dinner. It was so carefree.

Sabir Hussain

Chickens on the Milk Van

Well, I don't know whether that was halal or not halal, but they said it was halal. Most people bought their own chickens and did it their own way. The milkman used to bring them or we could go to poultry farms. There was plenty of meat in shops, but I didn't know if it was halal. The first shop in Huddersfield used to be on Sowood Street and it was called Kureshi General Store, that place was demolished when the Ring Road was built. Another shop called Punjab Stores opened after that one, this is still there in Springwood. Its been there since 1963.

Muhammad Ismail

Skin and Feathers

Because we didn't know if it was halal or not, so we used to get chickens from the farm and we would slaughter them by our own hands. We would put the skin and feathers into the fire, it was a coal fire then. It was very difficult. Some halal meat started to come in after and it was only Bullars shop at the time.

Hanif Asad

Asian Food

In those days, if you wanted any Asian food you had to cook it at home. There were no takeaways or very few takeaways where you could buy Asian food. You had to go down to Thornton Lodge to buy Asian food, but then gradually as time went on people started buying shops on Blacker Road in Birkby. Actually, there was just one grocery shop there and then others opened up. A Halal store eventually opened up later on, and then other people followed.

Asghar Ali

Halal Meat and Spices

It must have been in the 60s because I remember when I was young and we lived at Longroyd Bridge, we used to go to Thornton Lodge to buy the meat. That's where everybody would go and buy their meat from, there wee very few Asian shops in Huddersfield at the time and it was difficult to get halal meat and spices.

Rehana Tanwir

Massala

When people came from India, you would ask them to bring some spices or you could get them from Bradford. There were no shops here where you could buy the spices from. In Bradford there were only two shops, Asian shops where you could get spices from and lentils and you'd go there after a month. This was around 1956.

Balwant. S. Sandhu

Chillies and spices were hard to find in Huddersfield. People often travelled to Bradford or ordered spices from relatives and friends returning from the Indian Sub-Continent.

The Brook Street Wholesale Market building was built in 1888 and renovated in 1980. The Open Market was a popular place to buy food and to socialise. It is still popular with the Asian community for its Monday and Thursday markets, where you will find an array of Asian clothes and accessory stalls.

Only Two Places to Shop

There used to be a green grocers shop in the market. They had the English food, cauliflower, potatoes, carrots they had those things you couldn't get them from Woolworths. They were the only two places to do your shopping. The meat shop was in the market too, but we didn't know where to get it from at first, then we found out, so we'd get the meat from the market and there they'd have the chickens hung up. You would just ask for how many you needed and they'd get them down.

Baldev Singh

Chapter Eight

Community, Culture & Religion

Mayor H. F. Brook and the Pakistani High Commissioner open's the Pakistani Community Centre, Huddersfield, 1961. Photo courtesy of the Huddersfield Examiner.

Where are you from?

Even the ones before me they were really happy to see other Pakistanis, Indians. They would meet them happily and ask strangers things like, where are you from? how is everyone here and back home? It was like meeting up with your family.

Balqees Akhtar Ali

85

Community

Men Only

The community used to hire a hall and we'd go there. There were a couple, one on Manchester Road. My wife joined with me in 1964 and they didn't come in to the hall only the men went. In the hall we prayed and after that we celebrated. Today there are so many Muslims in Huddersfield there isn't one big hall for them, they've split into different mosques. To fit them all in you'd need a very big hall, and there just isn't one big enough!

Muhammad Ismail

The First Eid

There was a small mosque two miles from our house. There weren't many people going to Friday prayer because we worked seven days and seven nights, so we couldn't wake up to go to Friday prayers, but there was a small house where the mosque was. I remember the very first Eid I was here for and I set off for Eid prayer. First of all I couldn't find the place where the Eid prayer was because they didn't have Eid prayer at the mosque, they hired a church hall and I didn't know that. When I found it, I had missed the Eid prayer. The second year exactly the same happened, because before Eid, our shopkeepers used to deliver groceries and leave a leaflet in our houses which was by the mosque committee telling you were it was going to be held. After that, I made sure I asked somebody where it was going to be held and I haven't missed an Eid prayer since.

Karam Hussain

Community Halls

We used to hire a hall out. Not so many people prayed then, they were young and very busy. You'd probably read at home and then in the mosques, but we'd rent a hall for Eid. There was one in Thornton Lodge, St. Patricks Hall where Eldon Electricals is now and we hired the Army Regiment building near the university behind the church. We even rented out the Vent Street, West Indian club, we've prayed in there and the Media Centre, we hired a few out over the years. There were a few people who got together to hire these hall and they'd arrange it for us to celebrate Eid.

Hanif Asad

Blackpool

We went to Blackpool once and we were having a nice time having, donkey rides and swings and all sorts. We went and had fish and chips and salads, the lot. We were enjoying ourselves so much we forgot we had no petrol in the car and near Halifax our petrol was gone! It was Sunday and on Sunday there was no garage or petrol pump open, so we sat in the car and slept, and the police car came, he asked, "What are you doing?" and we told him, "we have no petrol and we need to go to Huddersfield." He siphoned petrol from his car to give us petrol and he said, "next time be careful." It shows they were so relaxed, there were no qualms. They helped us a lot. Honestly, society was totally different then.

Sabir Hussain

The Avon Minx and cars in general were novel items for children. Photo taken in Lockwood, 1967.

Pick-ups and Drop-offs

Very few people used to have cars in those days because it was regarded as a waste of money. People used to share things more then, than they do now. If a person had a car and somebody wanted to go somewhere they would just simply ask and they would take them. If a relative was coming to London from Pakistan, they would come to Heathrow airport and you would ask somebody who's got a car if they would take you to pick them up. They would go out of their way to make arrangements to go and collect that person and then you'd just simply pay for the petrol. They'd be quite happy with that.

Asghar Ali

Traditional Indian Elephant carving can be seen at Melas across Yorkshire. Huddersfield Mela, renamed Worlds Together, was first held in 1988 in Greenhead Park.

The First Mosque

Upper George Street mosque, it was a house that the community bought and we started praying there... that's how the first mosque was set up.

Hanif Asad

Mela

Mela, I was an elected member at the time and I helped to get it established. It was set up for the people who were just coming into England and a way for people without families here to get to know the community. It was a community festival and I went to see the Director of Services at the time to see if they would be interested in an event like this and they were and it started in 1988. There was a Mela in Leeds and other people started celebrating things like St. Patrick's day and other events, so our people asked why we didn't celebrate our festivals and that was the thing that pushed for the Mela in Huddersfield.

Jamil Akhtar

Living in Asia

We can even say that we are living in Pakistan or India, as sometimes in some areas there are so many people who live there from the same area or the same village that they were from back home.

Karam Hussain

Culture

Traditions

Our culture and system is very old and famous. We used to go to toilet and use a water bottle to wash, that was different here. This was our culture not the British culture. Men and women went into clubs and pubs, but not Asians, Muslims, it was different for us. People used to say why don't you come to the pub and the club, you see, it was just different. We had grown up with different cultural traditions.

Mohammad Ismail

Punjabi Rackets

Upper George Street used to run all the way down to the Bus Station. Spring Street where Punjab Stores is, I think it was established 1963, it used to run straight down to the Bus Station too, where you pick people up and I used to live there on 9 Spring Street, in centre of town. I remember when we played Punjabi rackets, they'd be played very loud on the turntables, you could here them all the way down to Woolworths.

Hanif Asad

Stay at Home

In our tradition when the eldest son gets married, the tradition is to stay at home with the wife and mother and the dad, because its very rare that you here of, it probably does happen, but very rarely do you here of an elderly Asian woman or man being taken to a residential or nursing home, because there's always someone in the house and you've got to. It's just like they've brought you up so in return you've got to look after them in their old age.

Jasvindar Kaur

Integration

In those days, people like me who thought they were a bit educated, I think they tried to integrate into the English community, but at the time it was also important to know about your own culture.

Balvinder Kaur

Asghar and Balqees, newly weds. Woodthorpe Terrace, 1974.

Deaths and Marriages

We have maintained the culture, say in weddings you will see we have hundreds of people at the wedding and the same if someone dies, everyone will come to pay their respects. Our culture is very community based.

Karam Hussain

"Uncle, I've never seen your face."

My brother had died and he had a daughter in India. I rang her and she was crying saying, "Thia uncle, I have never seen your face." She was getting married, so I said I would pay for her wedding and give her away. It was a strange thing going into a family, my brother's family and seeing he had a grown up daughter who I'd never seen before.

Baldev. S. Gill

Photo of a young family in Pakistan, 1958.

92

Balqees on her wedding day; 1974.

Mix of cultures

My parents would always say to me that when you were eighteen you would go back to India to get married. So I didn't mind, I knew that was the tradition and I was proud to be Indian.

Jasvindar Kaur

Two Languages

At home parents insisted that we spoke Punjabi because we spoke English amongst ourselves and they were really worried that we wouldn't be able to speak our mother tongue fluently, if we were speaking with people who couldn't speak English; friends and relatives. So we grew up in two languages.

Mehboob Khan

Religion

Learning Arabic

There was only one Mosque in Upper George Street and everybody used to go there to pray. You'd go to the mosque to say the Friday prayer and to read the Eid or if guests came over the weekend. You'd go when you had time basically and to send the children to learn the Quran. Even when we were young we used to go. In those days, it was difficult because we lived in Lockwood and in order to learn the Quran there were some classes after school which were held in Upper George Street Mosque. My brother and I had to catch the bus in the evening and I remember the bus fare was something like 2p to get from Lockwood to town. We had trolley buses in those days as well. That was quite a trek because we used to go by ourselves because our dad was at work and then we used to come back at around seven or eight in the evening by ourselves on the bus. During winter it used to get dark early, so it wasn't always a nice journey.

Asghar Ali

Ramadhan

I remember Ramadhan came in 1963, it arrived in December. We would eat something at night and would sleep all day, and when we got up at four 'o'clock it was time to open the fast. I worked night shift work and in that month I managed to save enough money to go back to Pakistan...that was my fast!

Hanif Asad

Masjid Omar, Blacker Road, Birkby

Inside Guru Nanak Gurdwara, Sikh Temple. Prospect Street, Springwood.

Sikh Temple

We went to the Sikh Temple to learn Punjabi and to write it. I liked it. I got to meet other children, Sikh children got to find out about my religion and my background, I even met some friends there that I'm still friends with today. But the teachers were sometimes a bit harsh though, you got a ruler across your hand if you didn't behave.

Jasvindar Kaur

Children and Mosque

I took my children to the mosque to teach them Quran. I prayed at home, but taught my children what Islam is through the mosque, so they could teach their children and pass on our religion.

Balqees Akhtar Ali

95

Closeness to God

I think the difference from then and now is that in those days people were still very close to God and churches were filled. When we went to the church, when I was fifteen years old, at Christmas in church there wasn't space to sit because it would get so full, people were standing outside. Over the years, I have found that people seem to have drifted away from God and we seem to be going more towards worldly things; they're not as full as they were then.

Yaqub Masih

St. Cuthberts Church, Birkby.

Migrants from South-Asia came to Britain with four faiths; Islam, Sikhism, Hinduism and Christianity. Mosques and Temples were initially set up within community bought houses in the 1960s, to be used for the place of worship. Fifty years on, places of worship for these faiths are now visible across Huddersfield, in the shape of Mosques, Temples and shared Churches.

Masjid-e-Noor, Crosland Road,
Huddersfield was opened in 1979.
The Methodist Church building,
dates back to 1933 and closed in 1977.

Chapter Nine

Identities

A day out to Greenhead Park, 1975

First Home

I was born in India, but soon after my parents went to a place which is now Pakistan. My culture and my background is Pakistani. The culture in England now is fifty-fifty. We still remember our Pakistani culture, but we recognise the English culture too. I still love Pakistan, but it is my second home now and England is my first.

Mohammad Ismail

Achievements

I never even thought of going back to be honest with you, its better living such as working and income over here, there's nothing that I could do there. If I was committed in achieving something there I could have gone back, but I didn't even think of it. The facilities we have over here are advanced, they don't have that there and living standards are more comfortable. If I was still there I would be a farmer. There are a lot of things we have achieved here that we could not have done there.

Karam Hussain

British Asian

I was born in Pakistan, so my roots would be in Pakistan, although when I go back now it's become a totally alien place to me. It's a nice enjoyable place for a holiday, but that's it. If I were to go and live there I don't think I could cope, because I've become so accustomed to the British way of life that although I regard myself as an Asian, I'm British Asian. It's difficult to go back and adapt. If my father hadn't made that sacrifice of selling everything and taking the risk of coming here, I might not be in a position where I'm able to give the best to my children. My children have grown up and they have all become successful in their careers and I think that's basically down to my parents, taking that sacrifice and bringing us here and then giving us the best opportunity that they could.

Asghar Ali

Background

That is the advantage of living in Huddersfield, where you could have the two cultures and you just integrated. I'd like to keep the Asian influence and don't want to lose it, it's a very strong part of us we will always carry our colour with us and with that colour we should carry some of the culture. There's no reason why we should lose our identity just because we have come to another country. It's important that we understand where we are from.

Mamuna Karim

100

A Change

I go every year to see my relatives in Pakistan and we stay there for two months each time. When I came here, I went back to Pakistan after 15 years. At that time the wage wasn't very good and I couldn't afford to go, but now I prefer here because my children are here. I came here in 1960, I'm 81 now and I've been here fifty years, most of my life. So my wife and I go back to Pakistan just for a change.

Ashraf Ali

Wedding Bharat, Pakistan, 1963.

Home of my Parents

Pakistan is the home of my parents, I like both. If I'm here, I like it here if I'm there I like it there. You have to fulfil your days.

Shamim Begum

Going Back

Now I go back every year for three or four months and when I go back I feel alone, becauce my family is all here. We have a big house, a farm, a car in India, we have everything, but I still feel alone when I go there. You have to choose your home where you live. I have lived here for fifty-four years, all of my good life. It is an easier life here than in India; we have a gas cooker, electricity, fridge it's not a problem there, but this is home. The first time we went back was after twelve years because we were looking after the children and the second time it was twelve years again, because we were working. Now we sometimes go twice a year, but we can't live there for long because we are used to it here.

Balwant. S. Sandhu

Belonging

This is our home, this is where we belong. I go back every year to India and I am a stranger in my own country, I don't feel comfortable because I am missing home, missing this land, my children, grandchildren. I didn't go to India for nearly thirty years and now this is my home... but I am Indian because of my roots and that's where I was born.

Baldev. S. Gill

Huddersfield, view of Emley Moor Mast, dates back to 1956.

Glossary

Bharaat – A South-Asian groom procession to the wedding; consisting of groom, family and friends. Bhar-at, the Hindi name of India.

Chappatti - A flat, unleavened bread from northern India and Pakistan; also known as roti. A tandoori roti is a type of naan bread accompaniment.

Curry - is a generic description used throughout European culture to describe a general variety of spiced dishes, best known in South Asian cuisines, especially Indian cuisine. In Pakistan and North India, curry is usually referred to as saalan.

Daal - Lentils. Curry dish made with lentils.

Eid – A Muslim religious festival. The two Eids; Eid ul-Fitr commemorates the passing of the month of fasting, Ramadan. Eid an Arabic term to mean festivity and Fitr meaning to break fast and Eid ul-Adha, which last three days following Hajj; referred to as 'Big Eid'.

Eid Prayer (salah) - is performed in congregation at mosques during the morning of the religious festival of Eid.

Friday Prayer - also known as jum'ah is a congregational prayer that Muslims hold every Friday, just after noon in lieu of dhuhr (Zohr) prayer time.

Gulaam – South Asian term used to describe a servant.

Gurdwara – also known as Sikh Temple. Meaning the Gateway to the Guru, is a place of worship for Sikhs.

Halal - meaning lawful or legal to a Muslim. A term designating any object or an action which is permissible to use or engage in, according to Islamic law. Often used with regards to foods that can be eaten, based on the proper methods of slaughtering (to halal) an animal.

Holy Book - Religious texts, also known as scripture, are the texts which various religious traditions consider to be sacred, or of central importance to their religious tradition

Masjid - Muslims often refer to the mosque by its Arabic name, masjid. A mosque is a place of worship for followers of Islam. The word mosque in English refers to all types of buildings dedicated for Islamic worship.

Massala - Traditional spices used for cooking. Indian spices include chilli powder, garam massala and tumeric.

Mela - is a Sanskrit word meaning 'gathering' or 'to meet' or a Fair. It is used in the Indian subcontinent for all sizes of gathering and can be religious, commercial, cultural or sports. South Asian diaspora communities wishing to bring something of that tradition to their new countries has influenced the formation of yearly Melas across Britain.

Nannie – Urdu term used when referring to a persons' 'Nan'. A mothers' mum; grandmother.

Quran - is the central religious text of Islam, also sometimes transliterated as Qur'ān, Koran. Muslims consider the original Arabic Quranic text to be the final revelation of God.

Ramadhan - A holy month of fasting for Muslims. Urdu term for ramadhan is *ros-ay*. Also know as fasting.

Thia - Uncle; father's older brother.

Ashraf Ali and family, 1972.